CONGRATS!

TO:

FROM:

ALL THE GOOD

DOING LIFE AFTER THE DIPLOMA

DEXTERITY
NASHVILLE

DEXTERITY

Dexterity, LLC
604 Magnolia Lane
Nashville, TN 37211

Printed in the United States of America.

First edition: 2021
10 9 8 7 6 5 4 3 2 1

ISBN: 978-1-947297-28-9 (hardcover)
ISBN: 978-1-947297-29-6 (eBook)

Title: All the good : doing life after the diploma.
Description: Nashville, TN: Dexterity, 2021.
Identifiers: 9781947297289 (hardcover) | 9781947297296 (eBook)
Subjects: LCSH Life—Moral and ethical aspects. | Values. | Benevolence. | Success. | Self-actualization (Psychology) | Wisdom. | Conduct of life. | BISAC SELF-HELP / Motivational & Inspirational | SELF-HELP / Personal Growth / Success | SELF-HELP / Affirmations
Classification: LCC BJ1581.2 A44 2021 | DDC 158.1—dc23

Book and cover design by Sarah Siegand.
Original illustrations by Alli Hoffer and Ezra Siegand.

WHETHER WALKING THE STAGE VIRTUALLY OR IN PERSON,
YOU ARE THE BUILDERS, THE DOERS, THE DREAMERS.
YOU WILL INSPIRE AND CHANGE THE WORLD.

HATS OFF TO GRADS EVERYWHERE.

DO ALL THE **GOOD** YOU CAN,
BY ALL THE **MEANS** YOU CAN,
IN ALL THE **WAYS** YOU CAN,
IN ALL THE **PLACES** YOU CAN,
AT ALL THE **TIMES** YOU CAN,
TO ALL THE **PEOPLE** YOU CAN,
AS **LONG** AS EVER YOU CAN.

– John Wesley

CONTENTS

DO ALL THE GOOD YOU CAN

Your work has paid off—you've graduated! You've gained knowledge and friends, memories and experiences, and you're heading into a new season of life. As a new graduate, your head is full of knowledge you'll use in your work or in further education. Your heart's full of the pride and excitement of all you've accomplished. Looking back on the person you were a few years ago, would you have imagined the growth you see in yourself now? Would you have guessed at the opportunities and adventures your life has held as you've worked toward this moment? During the past few years, you've established new relationships, found new hobbies, and discovered new ideas that have inspired and challenged you. This has surely been an incredibly rich and exciting (and sometimes overwhelming) experience!

Now you're off on a new adventure. Whatever you plan to do after graduation, it will be different from your life the past several years. You'll learn to adjust to all kinds of new things, new places, and new people. You know you can do it. The people around you know you can do it. The world is ready and waiting for you. The real question for you now is encompassed in the first word of the quote at the beginning of this book— "do." What will you *do* with all that you've achieved? How will you use your life to make a positive mark on the world? A timeless piece of wisdom offers simple advice: Do all the good you can.

But what does "good" mean? Curing cancer? Solving world hunger? Bringing peace to a troubled planet? As we look at the world into which you are embarking, there is a lot of good that needs to be done. We can see that, though our world is an amazing and beautiful place, we are facing many problems. Humans are capable of incredible feats of body and mind, but tend to start fighting when challenged. Our planet is full of plants and animals of every shape and color, but many are facing an uncertain future because of climate change and extinction. Knowing all you know about our world, how will you approach it in order to do real good? You may be a scientist with the ability to cure cancer, or you may offer comfort to a friend who is fighting it. You may be an agricultural expert who knows how to end hunger, or you may contribute to a food bank in your community. You may be a world leader who can bring warring nations to peace, or you may bring a spirit of peace and calm to those you encounter.

Good comes in big actions and small efforts. Good cannot be restrained by definition, because the need for it is constant and ever-evolving. Consider the things you thought were good when you were a small kid. Maybe it was getting a sticker at the doctor's office or a piece of candy at school. Do those things mean the same to you now? Perhaps not, but they are still good! Good doesn't stop growing as you get older. The next years of your life will hold all

> EVERY THOUGHT YOU PRODUCE, ANYTHING YOU SAY, ANY ACTION YOU DO, IT BEARS YOUR SIGNATURE.
>
> —THICH NHAT HANH

kinds of surprises and challenges. You are prepared to take on them all. The good you encounter will astonish and stagger you. But the good you create will strengthen and empower you for all that will confront you as you journey through life. You—yes, you—are a force for good in the world.

One challenge for many new graduates is leaving behind the grading system. Teachers and professors score assignments to let you know whether they were good. You may even get feedback on parts of your work that were better than others, allowing you to understand how to make more of your work good. As a student, much of your life revolved around a grading system, watching for updates on completed assignments and trying to predict the best possible outcome. Students stay up late finishing papers, collaborating on group works, and cramming for exams. You've had the elation of receiving good grades and the woe of the not-so-good score. You've followed syllabi throughout the semesters. You've read countless books and articles. You've probably even begged an instructor for a little more time to complete your work once or twice. The grading system has been a constant in your life as a student.

Now that you've graduated, you will have to judge your work in the world for yourself. If you continue your education, you'll have a new grading system. If you go on to a job, you'll have reviews and feedback from a supervisor. As an adult in the world, you will have to grade your presence in the world. Although grades on tests and exams are good in the sense of sufficient or competent, the good you will now seek focuses on virtue, commendable actions, and loyal relationships.

In some ways, your good work will turn inward. Instead of seeking good grades, you will seek to grade yourself as good. Though this is something others may try to do for you, ultimately you are the only person able to make this journey. As you move into life, you will continue to develop your moral compass, the inner voice that tells you what actions and attitudes are best for you and your community. You will have the ability to accept, reject, or explore things you believed as a younger person. You will find people and communities that will help you as you work on being good in the world. As a graduate, the work is up to you!

In the coming years, you will explore your vocation, occupation, and profession. This is the natural and expected next step for new graduates. But do those words just mean the same thing: what you do for a living? These words are often used interchangeably, but as we explore doing good, it's important to understand the differences between them.

Throughout your life, you may have several iterations of vocation, occupation, and profession. There are those rare folks who know exactly what their dreams and skills are, who sail through their educational journey and land their dream job. Some people know what they want to do in life from childhood. We all know someone who has their mind set on a particular vocation and then achieves it. Then there are those who explore, experiment, and find their passion along the journey. Understanding the difference among vocation, occupation, and profession can help you navigate doing good in each as you go forth.

First, the word *vocation* shares a root with the word *vocal*. The Latin root means "to call." Vocation is sometimes used in a religious context, like when people feel called by God to serve in a role in a church or community. But many people feel called to a line of work or to a passion. Your vocation may or may not be how you make a living, but it is a big part of how you make your life. A vocation may be a calling to play music or create art, something that speaks to your soul and gives you deep satisfaction. Your vocation may call you to serve in your community or be a part of a social action network.

However you live out your vocation, you can be sure that it will add to the good in the world. If you enjoy playing music, you know the joy it brings to those who listen (and maybe sing along). If you enjoy sports, you know about camaraderie and friendly competition. If you enjoy volunteering, you've experienced the appreciation of the recipient of your work as well as the gratification in your own heart. These are all examples of the good of vocation.

Next is the word *profession*. It brings to mind professional athletes, professional writers, or professional artists. We draw a line between professional and amateur based on the difference of being paid or not, but this isn't necessarily the best comparison. In medieval times, there were only three professions: medicine, law, and divinity. Now we use the term to apply to any pursuit that requires extensive training or study.

Over the centuries, more and more professions have been recognized, but all share the common feature of being an intellectual pursuit that requires years of education or training. So, understanding this definition, a professional football player would be someone who has spent many years learning and perfecting their performance in the sport. Another way to understand profession is in the context of a discipline. What study or training are you disciplining yourself to achieve? Though an athlete and an attorney have different types of training for their professions, both must be disciplined.

The word *occupation* is often used in place of *profession*, but there are some important distinctions between the two. The root of *occupation* is *occupy*. What occupies your time? How do you spend the majority of your time? Occupation is more of a neutral or generic term than either vocation or profession. In completing forms, we are often asked to fill in our occupation.

This question is not asking about our call in the world (vocation) or what we are studying to become (profession), but is simply a general term regarding our work.

Your occupation may be a salesperson or student. An occupation is no less important than a vocation or a profession and is a good way to do good in the world. Even if your current occupation is temporary or not your final goal, you can do good in it! Think of the ways people have shown you goodness while performing their occupation. Maybe it was a barista who complimented you during your coffee run or a grocery clerk who asked you about your day. These are small examples of the ways people in any occupation can do good, and you can, too.

> THE SMALLEST ACT OF KINDNESS IS WORTH MORE THAN THE GRANDEST INTENTION.
>
> —OSCAR WILDE

The terms we're exploring—*vocation*, *profession*, and *occupation*—are all distinct, but interrelated. Imagine a Venn diagram of these terms. There would be a circle for each of these words, and they would overlap in four places. Each term would overlap with one other (vocation and profession, profession and occupation, occupation and vocation). Then, in the middle of the image, all three would overlap. As you take the next steps on your post-graduation journey, you will find yourself in places that overlap and places that do not. That's okay! We are multifaceted individuals and can have different vocations, professions, and occupations. As you go through life, you will find yourself in different parts of that diagram—sometimes overlapping, sometimes not. But wherever you are, you have the opportunity to do good. You can do good with your vocation, with your profession, and with your occupation. The opportunities are endless; you just have to look for them!

Whatever roads you choose, you must cherish and protect your personal integrity. Integrity is the practice of doing what is right and showing a strong moral foundation. In philosophy, it's defined as honesty and truthfulness, accuracy in your actions, impeccability in speech. In short, it's sticking to what's right and being reliable in that. Integrity is when your "yes" means yes and your "no" means no. Having integrity will get you far, because people will know they can trust you and count on you to follow through.

In relationships, you build integrity each day. Having integrity can also mean that you must stand up for yourself and others in ways that are uncomfortable or that go against the crowd. Sometimes integrity feels like standing up against the crowd or doing the right thing when nobody's watching.

Whether you realize it or not, integrity is something you value in your mentors and in your closest friends. If you prize your integrity and make decisions that show it, your vocation, profession, and occupation will be all the better. And your ability to do good will multiply.

All of the questions that lie ahead on your journey of doing good may feel vast and insurmountable. Together, we will explore the who, what, when, where, and how. We'll pose questions and share stories that will enlighten and inspire you. Your moral compass will guide you throughout your life, and now is a good time to decide how you'd like it to be set. The quote we are exploring will help you calibrate your compass and point you in the direction of doing "all the good you can" as you start this next journey.

BY ALL THE MEANS YOU CAN

Doing good happens in many different ways. Our first exploration focuses on the "means" of doing good. But what does that mean exactly? Does means equal money? Are only those who have a lot of money able to access means? Absolutely not. In this case, *means* is a synonym for *strategy* or *plan*. Money can be part of that plan, but having a bigger vision is what really matters when doing good "by all the means you can." What kind of strategy or plan do you want to make for doing good throughout your life?

Consider the example of Oseola McCarty. Born in 1908 in Hattiesburg, Mississippi, she was raised by her mother, aunt, and grandmother, who all worked as washerwomen. When Ms. McCarty was in sixth grade, she had to leave school to care for an ailing aunt and was never able to return to her studies. Instead, she spent almost seventy-five years taking in laundry, which she washed by hand to earn a living. She used a washboard, clothesline, and iron—no fancy machines. Ms. McCarty loved working and described those years not as demanding and difficult, but as fulfilling and meaningful.

Ms. McCarty was committed to saving as much as she could, and when she retired in 1996, those few dollars saved each week for decades totaled approximately $280,000. That may not seem like a large sum in today's world, but it's how she used the money that's the real story. She decided the best use for her money was to endow a scholarship at the local university, the University of Southern Mississippi. People were so inspired by the generous and visionary means with which Ms. McCarty invested, that the scholarship fund quickly tripled and has since put numerous students through school. Although her life was humble, her saved pennies will continue to change lives through the scholarship endowment.

Ms. McCarty did a lot of good in her occupation as a laundress. She took in dirty clothes and made them perfect for their next wearing. After her death, one of her customers kept the last shirt she had laundered for him in his closet, unworn, as a reminder of her dedication to her occupation. It was clean, crisp, and perfectly pressed—a testament to her skill. Ms. McCarty also used her vocation as a means for good. Her love for her community and dedication to the next generation inspired her gift to the university. She allowed her passion for her neighbors to be a force for good that will allow her to be remembered for many, many years to come.

> DO A LITTLE BIT OF GOOD WHERE YOU ARE. IT IS THOSE LITTLE BITS OF GOOD PUT TOGETHER THAT OVERWHELM THE WORLD.
>
> —DESMOND TUTU

Other people find their means for good through their vocation. While studying to become a lawyer, Bryan Stevenson took a class on race and poverty litigation and worked at an organization that represented death row inmates in the South. Originally from Delaware, Mr. Stevenson was shocked to see the high rates of incarceration among black men in Alabama. He was especially concerned about disparities in death row sentencing. Since the United States Congress eliminated funding for death-penalty defense, many poor and minority defendants were unrepresented in court. In the early 1990s, Mr. Stevenson started the Equal Justice Initiative in Montgomery, Alabama, which provides counsel to anyone in the state sentenced to death row and has overturned countless wrongful cases. He has challenged court race and class biases and championed more just treatment for children in the judicial system. Mr. Stevenson has used his education and work as a means for change on personal and systemic levels.

As you think about what your means may look like, think about the things Ms. McCarty and Mr. Stevenson have in common. Although their stories may feel completely opposite, the two share a strong work ethic, passion for their communities, and vision for the future. They both approached their daily work with pride and care, while simultaneously setting their sights on the impact they could make in the future. Although she passed away in 1999, Ms. McCarty was able to meet the first recipients of her scholarship. Her fund continues to pave a brighter future for promising students.

Meanwhile, Mr. Stevenson continues to practice law and wrote a book about his work establishing the Equal Justice Initiative. That book, *Just Mercy: A Story of Justice and Redemption*, was adapted into a movie in 2019. His work continues, and his example of advocacy will remain powerful to future generations.

This brings us to the importance of recognizing both vocation and avocation. At this

> PEOPLE SAY, "WHAT IS THE SENSE OF OUR SMALL EFFORT?" THEY CANNOT SEE THAT WE MUST LAY ONE BRICK AT A TIME, TAKE ONE STEP AT A TIME.
>
> —DOROTHY DAY

point in your life, you are probably hyper-focused on your vocation or principle occupation. What job will you do? What studies do you need to undertake to be successful in that job? Are there additional degrees and certificates and licenses and stamps and merit badges needed? It can be overwhelming to consider all that will go into your chosen career and the many years ahead to practice it. For some, you've felt a calling to a specific profession your whole life. If that's not you, it can be easy to feel jealous of that certainty!

For others, exploring options and getting a sample of many different things is appealing.

However you do it, everyone is expected to pick a career or vocation. That's why it's important to remember that alongside your chosen vocation, you will have many avocations. What is an avocation? That's just a fancy word for hobbies or extracurricular activities. You know, the things you enjoy doing in your spare time. These, too, can be a means for doing good in the world.

For example, Ms. Oseola McCarty worked diligently as a laundress, but in her spare time she loved to sit and chat with friends and study the Bible. In 2020, a memorial to honor her legacy was erected at the University of Southern Mississippi. It consists of two vintage-style lawn chairs. One for you, the visitor, and one occupied by a statue of Ms. McCarty wearing her Sunday dress and holding her Bible. Imagine the good she did from that chair! Chats with neighbors about the weather,

> I CANNOT DO ALL THE GOOD THAT THE WORLD NEEDS. BUT THE WORLD NEEDS ALL THE GOOD THAT I CAN DO.
>
> —JANA STANFIELD

advice to friends about their troubles, reminiscing with family members.

We are not meant to be one-dimensional beings, caring only about making money. Sure, we need to be able to take care of ourselves and our families, but there is more to life! Throughout your life, you've probably already had several avocations. Did you play soccer or sing in a choir? Were you interested in visual art or exploring nature? All of these count as avocations and are certainly a means of doing good. If you played a sport as a child, there were adults who volunteered to teach you the skills and rules. They spent their Saturday mornings with a bunch of high-energy kids, finding ways to channel that energy into a game. They probably bought the juice boxes too. Looking back on those experiences, you'll agree that those volunteers were doing some major good!

Not all of us have the patience and skill to coach youth sports, but we all have interests and hobbies that can lead us to doing good. This is a means of doing good that doesn't rely on finances, but just on willingness and time—two things we can all make happen. Look around your community. Are there groups doing work that you find interesting and important? Are there needs that are unmet? Your time and talent may make all the difference!

Your "means" may be just a few hours a month or a couple of times a year, and that's fine. You don't need to establish a new group or lead a new movement. You can put "all the means you can" into action in small and meaningful ways now. And, as your heart finds its joy, you can invest more deeply. You may find a lifelong passion in something unexpected. Keep your eyes and heart open to new means of doing good in the world around you.

We each have different advantages, and how you use those advantages can be a means for good. Privilege is a form of power or benefit that is tied to social group and identity. Having

or lacking privilege is a reflection of how power is distributed in our society and is generally outside of your control. Things like gender, race, sexual orientation, religious affiliation, wealth, and ability all impact your amount of individual benefit.

Think about your own assets. What things do you have to be thankful for? Again, these things are outside of your control and shouldn't be seen as embarrassing or shameful in any way. In examining your assets, you can appreciate all you've been given. Understanding your advantages in the world allows you to leverage them for the good.

Having privilege doesn't mean life has been easy or without struggle; it simply recognizes that we live in a highly stratified society. By seeing your own advantages and disadvantages clearly, you are able to bring awareness, listen, and speak up for others when they aren't being recognized.

For example, imagine that you're at a team meeting at work. The room is crowded with all the workers listening to management explain a new policy. They ask if there are any questions. Beside you is a colleague in a wheelchair. Your colleague has a question but can't be seen because the room is crowded. What would you do to use your privilege in this situation? Would you tell your colleague his hand can't be seen? Would you raise your hand as well to let the speaker know there's a question? Would you ask others to move aside so your colleague could take part in the conversation? Using your privilege as a means for good may require some self-examination and honesty, but it will provide you with another method for doing good.

While you were a student, you had opportunities to hone skills in many different areas. Though you may have focused on one particular major, field, or occupation, you took classes from many different departments and areas. Perhaps some of those were required classes that you steeled yourself to complete, but you gained knowledge and skills, nonetheless. Those hard-earned skills can be means for good in your life. Perhaps some of those required classes exposed you to new ideas that will become part of your vocation, or call, in life. Maybe they stirred up a passion for literature or mechanics or math. In most schools, there are core classes that everyone has to pass, regardless of their anticipated profession. Depending on your academic bent, some of those classes may have been more interesting to you than others. Some of you would rather read Shakespeare any day over solving algebra problems! But the exposure to new and different things makes everyone better. Consider the broad knowledge you've gained. What privilege does it give you? As a new graduate, you are perfectly poised to take that skill and insight and make it a means for good.

IN ALL THE WAYS YOU CAN

Doing good "in all the ways you can" sounds like an enormous undertaking. How in the world can anyone do good *always*? Are we supposed to be saints or angels every moment of our lives? We know that isn't likely to happen. But, in setting this high bar, we do have a lot to think about in terms of how we live our lives and what choices we make day by day and moment by moment.

First, let's discuss the kind of mindset needed to see the ways that we can do good. For many people, the world is binary—either this or that. From a young age, we are taught opposites:

black/white, short/tall, good/bad. This is an important step in learning language and developing cognition. However, as we mature, we begin to see that not everything can be so compartmentalized.

As a new graduate, you've certainly been challenged by this concept. You've had classes and teachers who have challenged you to see the gray areas in our world. You've read things that have opened the world in new and vibrant ways. You're ready and able to take a more nuanced approach to the world that goes beyond the binary. You can still see that some things are good and others are bad, but you no longer need such a simplistic worldview. You're able to use your education and experience to see the world in its multidimensional complexity. This is a both/and mindset, and it will take you far in doing good in all the ways you can. So, instead of looking at the world in either/or terms, you can now see that both/and can be true (and often is).

Understanding this gray area depends on the ability to hold tension and be a little uncomfortable. In trying your best to see all sides of an issue or event, you must acknowledge the various perspectives of the actors and see that they each have good intentions. This type of conflict of perspective can create tension, which can make you uncomfortable. Being able to hold that tension amid challenges is a way of doing good in the world. It halts your rush to judgment and gives you time to better evaluate situations. Once you begin living in the gray areas of the world, searching for new perspectives, and listening to others, you realize why so many folks prefer the good/bad binary—it's a lot easier! However, in just recognizing this tension, you're taking steps toward doing good.

In attempting to do good "in all the ways you can," you may also see that your view of good may not be good for everyone. Your perspective is couched in your identity, experience, and privilege in the world. In other words, your culture, race, gender, faith, wealth, etc. all create your perspective. Let me tell you about a time when someone's perspective was way off and how in resetting it, she was equipped to see things in a very different way.

For several years, a woman worked at a refugee resettlement agency doing mostly immigration work. Folks would go to the agency for help with green card applications, family reunification, and other immigration issues. She loved this work and the amazingly diverse community she served. Her office was on the second floor of the building, overlooking the front parking lot. Often, when she heard a car door shut, she would look out the window to see if it was the person or family she was expecting. Over the weeks and months of this window peeking, the woman noticed a trend that upset her. Many times, a man would get out of the driver's side of the car and then open the door to the backseat for his wife, mother, or other female relative. This really ruffled the woman's feathers. Why did they make the women sit in the back when there was no one else taking up the front passenger seat? Why were they relegated to the back like second-class citizens?

Each time the woman witnessed this through her perch behind the second-story window, she became more and more incensed over this perceived mistreatment. Then one afternoon a man whom she had known for a long time was in her office for an appointment. When they concluded the work he needed done, she got up her nerve and told him what she had witnessed over the months and her anger that these men weren't treating women as equals. He was quiet as he looked at her with a smirk. He saw right through her American perspective. "Friend," he said, "the back seat is the safest part of the car."

With that, her smug, judgmental perspective was challenged. The men that the woman had witnessed were doing something to ensure the safety of those they loved. As newcomers to our country, survivors of war and refugee camps, they were exercising a simple act to give them a sense of safety and security, a way to do good. With this insight, she began to see the world in a different (though imperfect) way. Instead of seeing something and judging it in a binary good/bad way, she practiced the both/and mindset. She evaluated her privilege. What else did she not know about what was happening? How could what was before her be a way of doing good in the world?

Using your education and experience, how will you challenge yourself to see more ways of doing good in the world?

As a new graduate, your future is beckoning with all the promises and challenges that await you. Using an expansive both/and mindset will allow you to engage in your community and the world in ways that will bring good. Think about the past week or so in your life. In what ways have you practiced good? Perhaps you picked up a piece of litter while walking at the park. Maybe you offered a smile and wave to the person holding a sign at an intersection. You've probably sent friends an encouraging text or just a "hi," so they knew they were in your thoughts.

In your vocational life, your ways to do good are innumerable, whether you are teaching children or selling groceries. You get to choose how you approach your work and the values you take with you. Are you the coworker who can always be counted on for a smile and a kind word? Are you the supervisor who takes time to acknowledge your employees? Perhaps you work with the public and must handle all kinds of issues with grace and patience. In your work life and in your personal life, you can choose to do good in ways large and small.

> AND NOW THAT
> YOU DON'T HAVE TO
> BE PERFECT, YOU
> CAN BE GOOD.
>
> —JOHN STEINBECK

For some, the idea of doing good is synonymous with charity. What images come to mind with that word? Do you think of Salvation Army bell ringers asking for donations at Christmas time? Perhaps your faith community or social organizations have organized giving for charity. Does charity have positive or negative connotations for you? On the positive side, it feels really good to give, whether it's a financial donation to a nonprofit group or an old coat from your closet. Many have given a stranger a dollar here and there, or given canned goods to a food bank. The world needs these acts of charity! But, as we apply our both/and mindset, is charity the only way to do good? Are the recipients of our giving really getting what they need? Are they being treated with dignity and worth?

John Wesley, author of the "all the good" quote, modeled ways of doing good by opening schools and clinics for the poor in England and encouraging his followers to give "all ... you can." He acted beyond just the basic needs of the poor in his community in order to bring about systemic change.

An old fable illustrates the difference between charity and systemic change and the need for both in the world. The story is set in a small village beside a river. One day, a person from the village was at the riverside and noticed a baby floating down the river. Without a second thought, the villager jumped into the river to save the baby.

By the time the villager grabbed the infant and swam back to shore, other villagers had gathered to help get the baby and their neighbor to safety. They checked the baby for injuries and wrapped it in a warm blanket, discussing who among them could care for the child. The next day, two babies came down the river, and the following day there were three. Soon, the entire village was caught up in the work of saving the babies—swimming against the rush of the river to get the babies, providing blankets and clothing, finding milk and food, tending to them through the night. The work was exhausting and used all the resources of the small village, but they kept working to save the babies because it was the right thing to do. Who would allow babies to drown if they could save them?

Then one day a brave young person announced that he was going on a jour-ney. He was going to

> WE HAVE A DUTY TO SHOW UP IN THE WORLD WITH MEANING AND PURPOSE AND A COMMITMENT TO DOING GOOD. AND TO USE ANY PRIVILEGE THAT WE HAVE TO MAKE POSITIVE CHANGE AND TO DISRUPT OPPRESSIVE SYSTEMS.
>
> —MEENA HARRIS

follow the rushing river upstream to find out what was happening to these babies. Why were they put in the river? Who or what caused this? He was going to find the cause of the problem and then find a solution.

The villagers in this tale did what we all imagine we would do—jump to the rescue, be the superhero, provide lifegiving care. These actions are great examples of charity: giving to solve the immediate need. Necessary stuff! But the young person who trekked upstream was seeking a different way to do good in this situation. He was seeking change to the systems causing the problem. What would the villagers find upstream? Perhaps there had been a natural disaster or a war that caused babies to be displaced. Maybe it was a terrible person. It was a brave thing to look upstream! And while they searched for a solution to the river of babies, the villagers would continue their life-saving work. There were two ways of doing good here, and both were necessary.

The charity of immediate care is vital, as is the longer-term systemic change needed to solve the problem. And you have the power to offer both.

A good example of creating system change is the Bill and Melinda Gates Foundation. We've all heard of Bill Gates and the computing empire he built, Microsoft. You've most likely used his software many times. By the time he was thirty-two years old, Bill Gates was on *Forbes* magazine's list of most wealthy people in the world. For over twenty years, he was considered the richest person in the entire world. He led Microsoft as CEO until 2000, when he stepped down to focus on philanthropy. It would be easy for an ultra-successful person like Bill Gates to approach philanthropy in a self-centered way. He could simply throw some money at some problems and walk away, still extraordinarily wealthy.

Instead, the Bill and Melinda Gates Foundation focuses on tackling the global problems that are ignored by governments and other organizations. They have made the intentional decision to be an upstream problem-solving organization. For example, one of the goals of the foundation is fighting poverty. Instead of simply giving charity to impoverished people, they have focused on improving healthcare, providing clean water and sanitation, and supporting the education of girls in developing countries.

You can see how these actions go upstream to fight poverty. In improving healthcare and access to vaccines, people are healthier and more able to work. In providing access to clean water and toilets, disease spread is reduced. In educating girls, more opportunities will be open to them when they become adults. In addition, Bill and Melinda Gates encourage their fellow billionaires to give away 97 percent of their wealth. They have plans for how their money will continue to do good in the world long after their deaths.

You have countless opportunities ahead to do good in ways big and small, in ways that are charitable and in ways that lead to systemic change. Your education gives you the foundation necessary to ask important questions and pursue creative solutions. You are able to see beyond the binary of good/bad to appreciate the nuanced nature of our world. You can appreciate the perspectives of those around you, ask questions for greater insight, and approach problems with curiosity and determination.

As you travel through life, you will find more and more ways of doing good in the world. You will find helpful ways to be charitable in your community and work toward the systemic change to address issues in your work, in society, and in the world at-large.

IN ALL THE PLACES YOU CAN

A popular gift for new graduates is Dr. Seuss's classic book, *Oh, the Places You'll Go!* You may have received a copy of this book or a card. Like Dr. Seuss's best material, it rhymes and inspires. "You're off to great places! Today is your day! Your mountain is waiting, so get on your way!" Dr. Seuss is often one of the first authors we read as children, so it's fitting that he sees grads off on the next adventure. Oh, the places you'll go, indeed.

You may already have places in mind that you plan to go. Often, starting a new job or the next level of education requires a geographic move. It's equal parts thrilling and scary to imagine life in a new place. Talk about holding tension—you can be brave and afraid, excited and worried, all at once. There are so many new opportunities to discover, new people to meet, new landscapes to explore.

At the same time, being separated from friends and family can be a daunting idea. Thankfully, technology has made long distances seem less vast since you can video chat and text with loved ones so easily. Still, it isn't the same as having your loved ones there for a hug.

As a young minister, John Wesley was asked to travel from his native England to the new colony of Georgia in 1735. In brief, it didn't go well—the native people he hoped to convert weren't receptive, the colonists weren't as religious as he'd hoped, and he fell in love with someone who spurned him. He stayed for just two years, leading a church for the new English settlers and preaching to the native people near Savannah. Wesley was a rigid person at this time in his life and, like other colonists of his time, felt that he could recreate England and English society in the New World. He was disappointed and confused that this wasn't the case.

Still, being in this new place, meeting new people, and having new experiences was transformational for Wesley, who went on to have quite a different perspective on his life's work. With that new mindset, he went on to lead revivals across England, and his theology became the foundation of the Methodist church.

Whether you travel across oceans or across town, the places you go throughout your life will transform you in ways you can't even imagine. Like Wesley's trip to America, things may not go as planned, and that's okay. Even the best-laid plans and intentions don't always work out. But the places you go will become part of your story, building in you wisdom and maturity. You'll have more chances to do good in all the places life takes you.

> IT'S YOUR ROAD AND YOURS ALONE. OTHERS MAY WALK IT WITH YOU, BUT NO ONE CAN WALK IT FOR YOU.
>
> —PAULO COELHO

As you reflect on all you've learned in school, you'll see the ways your teachers prepared you for work and further education. All those reading lists and lectures had a purpose! Your teachers have given you tools to use throughout your life.

You soaked up the information and learned the skills that you'll need as you venture out on the next steps. You are ready! So where will you go?

For some, you see your future playing out in your hometown, the place where you grew up and where your family has roots. For others, you imagine new vistas and places in other parts of the state, country, or world. You may imagine what life could be like in another place or feel a sense of peace and security with your familiar surroundings. Whatever your vision of "place," the important thing is that you are the one who is there and your ability to do good where you are doesn't change. It can be easy to fall into frustration or despair if you're not in the geographic location of your dreams. But don't lose sight of the present!

You are where you are for an abundance of reasons, and you can make it good. The key is to embrace the present while not giving up on your hopes and dreams for the future. Getting to the right place takes time, so don't let yourself be overwhelmed with yearning for a different place. Find out what you can do to make the place you are the best it can be.

Everyone knows what it's like now to have a long season in which people around the world are unable to travel freely. People have missed vacations, relocations, school and work opportunities, and time with family and friends. So many have wished to be in a different place. However, as difficult as it's been, life hasn't stopped. We may dream of a beach trip or traveling to a foreign country, but we've found ways to experience those places creatively. We've watched the waves lap the beach on a video feed or eaten food from a place far away. And as we're able to use technology to "be" in many different places virtually, there are many experiences we don't have to miss out on and places we can explore from our homes. In some ways, this pandemic has made the world a smaller place. The ways people have found to do good is amazing!

In Zambia, a country in southern Africa, a Catholic nun and public health advocate saw a place to help her country during the pandemic. Sister Astridah

Banda saw that all the notices about health and safety were in English. Although English is the official language of Zambia, over seventy languages are spoken throughout the country. Even though the steps to protect oneself from COVID-19 were simple, she was afraid that many in her country wouldn't know to wash their hands often, wear a mask, and practice social distancing.

To get the word out, Sister Banda took to the radio waves and hosted a call-in show for people to ask questions about the virus and staying safe. To be able to help the most people, she hosted her show in seven languages, easily bouncing from one to another depending on the comfort of the caller. Her creative approach has spread to neighboring countries and continues to share information in places other media doesn't reach.

I ENCOURAGE YOU TO LOOK FOR THE GOOD WHERE YOU ARE AND EMBRACE IT.

—FRED ROGERS

Another hero of the pandemic is Ethel Branch, a member of the Navajo Nation in Arizona. Ms. Branch was the attorney general of the Navajo Nation, but resigned from her job when she saw her community on the Navajo and Hopi reservations being infected with COVID-19 in record numbers. She knew that there were many people, the elderly in particular, who lived on the reservations without running water or electricity, two things critical in staying healthy and getting current information. In just a few short months, she was able to raise over five million dollars and mobilized her community. Residents with vehicles drove food to families in need. One father and son began delivering water to those without access to the utility. Ms. Branch's love for the place she lives and the people there inspired an entire community to do good in a critical time.

Like Sister Banda, Ms. Branch's deep connection to her community, to her place in the world, served as an instrument for doing good. Because they each know the people around them and their needs, they were able to act quickly in ways that outsiders couldn't. Each shows the value of connection to place.

As you look around your community, you'll be able to find stories of people doing good despite the situation. And, if you take time to be introspective, you'll find good that you've been able to do from where you are during challenging times.

What good were you able to do from your "place" in the COVID-19 pandemic? Were you able to see friends and family in person or offer greetings by phone or text? Did you find new and creative ways to connect with those you love? These simple acts of connection are so good, especially at a time when physical distance must be maintained. Though our bodies may be far apart, our hearts can connect.

An important aspect of "place" is the natural world wherever we are. Being connected to nature is grounding and good for our souls. It reminds us that we are part of the earth, just another species of mammal dependent on the intricate cycles of nature. Spending time outdoors in nature has been shown to lower stress and help our bodies heal. Whether it's untouched wilderness or a planned city park, going outside and breathing is a wonderful way to celebrate the places where we are. As you explore the outdoors, notice that nature, as wonderful as it is, can be messy: leaves scatter, animals poop, dead flora and fauna decompose.

In fact, naturalists have noticed a big difference between natural wooded areas and those that have been reforested. Many reforested areas are planted with single species of trees, making the space a monoculture. Plantings like this are often used to harvest timber, so the forests are laid out in perfectly straight, spaced lines so that machines can cut down the trees when they mature.

Imagine you're on a road that has a permaculture forest on one side and a human-planted forest on the other. As you travel down the road, you'll become mesmerized by the uniformity of the new forest, with trees all of one type planted in straight rows. It's an unsettling beauty, but there is little to no undergrowth between the rows of stately trees. On the other side of the road, you may not know what to look at first; it's a messy tangle of large and small trees, bushy undergrowth, and probably a wildflower or two. If you look closer, you'll see animals looking for food, bees carrying pollen from plant to plant. Stop and smell, and you will take in the richness of the earth as it decomposes. It's a gloriously messy and alive place, producing food and habitats and oxygen—all good things!

The place you are now may feel similarly messy. You may feel surrounded by a tangle of decisions to be made and work to be accomplished. Like the naturally wild forest, it can be overwhelming. You may yearn for a place that is orderly, organized, and predictable. That place may seem easier to navigate and without the obstacles you see before you now. It may seem like an easier place to do good with its open spaces and soothing uniformity, but you are in your current place for a reason, and the opportunities to do good are abundant. Just like the biodiversity of the natural forest, your place offers ways to connect with friends, with the larger community, and with the world.

As you begin to see that your current environment is alive with possibilities, your perspective will grow. With that growth, you will be able to hone in on the places your dreams are taking you. Will you see the potential in the journey ahead? As a new grad, the world is open to you, and you have the power to be a force for good anywhere you go. Where will your passions take you? How will you prepare now for what awaits you in the future? Your education has equipped you for so much! Where will you use that knowledge to bring good into the places you are? How do you imagine you can do good in all the places life will take you?

AT ALL THE TIMES YOU CAN

When you were a student, time was probably always on your mind. You counted the minutes left in class. You thought about the number of days you had to work on a project. You anticipated the months and weeks until graduation. But now, you've done it! All those minutes turned into days turned into years. As a little kid just starting school, those years seemed eternal, but you made it through. It's time to celebrate and reflect!

During your years of school, some days may have passed in the blur of busyness, but other moments probably stand out. Do you remember times when someone was especially kind to you at a difficult moment? Do you remember teachers and adults who took extra time to make sure you had what you needed? Were there friends who made an impact on you? Reflect on the good that was extended to you over the past years of school.

As you go into the next phase of life, how will you pay that goodness forward? How will you extend the goodness you've received in the past toward others in the future? How will you plan for and use both the present and the future to do good? Many say it, and I have experienced it to be true—time speeds up as you get older. As a child, months last for eons, and years stretch infinitely. But as you get older, those months fly by, and years feel like a moment.

Recently, a man was reminiscing about his childhood. He vividly remembered enjoying summer days at the local swimming pool as a young child. Sunshine, cool water, snacks. Lots of snacks. And when the lifeguards would blow the whistle for the rest break, even the snacks couldn't distract him from thinking about how many years were ahead of him until he was eighteen and could swim with the adults during the break. What a glorious thing to never have to get out of the pool! And how many long years he still had to wait.

Of course, once he was eighteen, he didn't care at all about swimming all day. He'd moved on to other things. But that feeling of the expansiveness of time from childhood stayed with him. As he grew older, time seemed to go faster and faster. What once seemed like an infinite resource became more and more precious. Your opportunities to do good pass with time, so it's important to seize each and every day and moment at your disposal to be good in the world. Carpe diem!

There is a Chinese proverb that may inspire you as you think about times to do good: "The best time to plant a tree was 20 years ago. The second best time is now."

As you consider doing good through time, you can make choices in the present that will impact the future. What do you think you could accomplish in thirty-seven years? Jadav Payeng is known as the Forest Man of India. In thirty-seven years, he was able to transform a barren sandbar in the Brahmaputra River

> WHY YOU?
> BECAUSE THERE IS
> NO ONE BETTER.
> WHY NOW? BECAUSE
> TOMORROW ISN'T
> SOON ENOUGH.
>
> —DONNA BRAZILE

into a forest. Mr. Payeng lives in a remote part of India and was distressed at seeing once verdant river islands turn into desolate sand bars. So, he began taking time each morning to cultivate a plant. He would wake early in the morning, before the sun, and take his boat out to the sandbar. Starting with bamboo and grasses, he moved on to trees of many species.

Today this river island is alive with flora and fauna of all kinds. Tigers and elephants swim across the shallow river to enjoy the lush forest Mr. Payeng has grown. When he first started this project, others thought he was crazy for spending time on something that seemed preposterous to them. Now he is celebrated as a conservationist and has won India's highest civilian honor. Mr. Payeng used time as his means of doing good, and his patience and perseverance paid off.

So, as you plan for the future, how will you incorporate doing good into those plans? Let's start by taking a global view of doing good through time. Our world is a beautiful and amazing place. You, just by being you, are part of the global ecosystem. This is a great honor, and it comes with great responsibility.

As you go forward after graduation, you have the ability to make decisions that will positively impact this world. Do you have a passion for plants and animals? Are you concerned about global warming and its effects? Perhaps you'll channel that passion into taking steps to protect the natural world and our environment. That can mean making long-term decisions for good, like choosing a career or hobby that focuses on maintaining a healthy planet. It may be as short-term as recycling that water bottle you just used. As part of this glorious world, we all have the chance to do good and positively affect the future of our planet.

Caring for nature may mean taking political action for you. You may choose to vote for candidates who support the causes that speak to your passion. You may even go further and advocate for new laws and regulations. This is doing good systemically. Your voice has power, and your ability to do good for our planet is only limited by your imagination.

On a more local scale, you may choose to do good by supporting local organizations. Every city and town has organizations that are doing good, and you can find one that matches your passion and vision for the future. This may take the form of volunteering to read with kids at your local elementary school or mentoring younger teenagers as they work toward graduation. As a new graduate, you have so much experience and wisdom to offer! When you do good by giving to those who are younger, your impact moves with them as they grow, and your good continues.

Your family may be another place to do good over time. Elders in your family may need your listening ear to share their life experiences or to voice their worries. They are proud of your accomplishments and want to hear about your plans for the future. Simply spending time in person, by phone, or on video chat means the world to those who have watched you grow. Letting them know you care about them is a real act of doing good. When you chat with the elders in your life, ask them about the good things that have happened to them and the good things they have done. You may be surprised at the wealth of wisdom and experience they have to offer!

From the global scale to the personal relationship, doing good has no bounds through time. Use your passions and education to reflect on the long-term and large-scale good you'd like to bring about. Are you pursuing a career that will do good for others? What do you need to equip yourself for that over the coming years? Making career plans is a form of doing good. Being intentional about your decisions will benefit you and those you impact for years and decades to come. Who has inspired you as you've been in school? Was there a teacher who helped you succeed? Think about the hours that person invested in you and the sum of that impact. Will those few hours turn into years of good you are able to do? The best thanks you can give those special folks is to follow your path and multiply their investment of good.

Earlier, we discussed the concept of charity and justice. How do those ideas relate to doing good in time? Charity is typically the immediate fulfillment of a need, like a meal or clothing. Charity is also given in many professions. Doctors and lawyers,

> **GOODNESS IS THE ONLY INVESTMENT THAT NEVER FAILS.**
>
> —HENRY DAVID THOREAU

for example, are often asked to see someone who is unable to pay for their services.

Charity is needed in the world, and there may be times when you're in need of a charitable act from someone. We can't discount the importance of charitable hearts and actions in doing good. But, at all times, we must consider what's going on upstream. We can't separate charity from justice, especially over time. It's a beautiful and gracious thing to provide meals to hungry folks, but we must also look at the systems and inequities that have created food insecurity for so many. If we don't delve into the causes of an issue, it will only get worse over time. Using the present time, we can do good by being aware and curious about how things have become the way they are, how problems have been caused, and then work to change them. That is a gift that time gives so that you may do good.

The woman mentioned previously, whose early career was spent in refugee resettlement, spent part of her time on sponsorship development. Most refugees enter our country with just what they can carry, and they're in need of material help (clothing, furniture, food, etc.) and community support as they begin this new journey. Churches and faith communities often volunteer to come alongside refugee families as they resettle, and the woman's job was reaching out to those who had experience doing this. One church group she spoke with remembered a family they had helped resettle over twenty years previously. They marveled at how this family overcame the language barrier and how hard the parents worked to provide for their children. But the church group said that family moved away and was never heard from again. The church had invested time into this family but felt hurt by their departure. This made the church unwilling to invest in another refugee family.

Several months later, the sponsor developer heard from one of the church members who excitedly told her that they were ready to sponsor another family. What had changed their mind? The church had started a campaign to raise money for a new organ. It was going to cost several thousands of dollars, and they hoped that they could raise enough as a community. Within a few days of the start of the campaign, they received a check for the full amount … from the family they had helped resettle decades prior. The note attached told the church that the family had been setting aside money over time to find a way to thank the people who helped them get a new start. They heard about the need for a new organ and knew this was the time to offer their thanks. They had been planning and waiting to do good at the right time, unbeknownst to the church.

> WHILE WE DO OUR GOOD WORKS LET US NOT FORGET THAT THE REAL SOLUTION LIES IN A WORLD IN WHICH CHARITY WILL HAVE BECOME UNNECESSARY.
>
> —CHINUA ACHEBE

This story speaks to the privilege involved in the concept of time. The church members and the refugee family perceived the right time to offer thanks quite differently. The church sought affirmation immediately. They wanted to know that they'd made a difference and were appreciated. The family was waiting until they could offer their thanks adequately, not just with words but with a meaningful gift. The two parties had very different expectations of the other, especially over time. As we approach doing good over time, how can we recognize different perspectives of when things need to happen?

As you work to do good in both the present and the future, you will find that there are times you need to rest. There are times you need to be the recipient of good. This can be a hard thing to admit to in our culture. We value strength and courage and carrying on despite bad times, but we need to learn to rest when it's needed. There's an old Jewish tale that gives us some perspective on doing too much all the time. "Rabbi Levi saw a man running in the street, and asked him 'Why do you run?' The man replied, 'I am running after my good fortune.' Rabbi Levi tells him, 'Silly man, your good fortune has been trying to chase you, but you are running too fast.'"

Are you outrunning your attempts to do good?

There will be times in life when you need to stop and rest. For you, this may take the form of a weekly sabbath, the occasional unplugging from social media, or time apart for self-care. These are all ways of doing good! Using your time to promote recovery, renewal, and revival in your own soul is vital. We are human *beings*, not human *doings*. Beings are natural and have cycles of sleep and wake, of productivity and fallowness, of bloom and fade. Doings are machines that continue at constant speeds with only the need for some oil or cleaning once in a while. Embrace your human being-ness and allow your brain, your body, and your soul to rest.

Goodness does not just flow outward from you, as a new graduate embarking into the world. Goodness also needs to flow toward you and within you. Learn to rest, not to quit. When you allow your reserves to dip too low, your ability to do good dips with it. Caring for yourself is a requirement for doing good.

Self-care, sabbath, and rest look different for different people. For those who are extroverts, time among family and

friends may be the boost needed for renewal. For introverts, time alone often does the same thing. Throughout your life's journey, what you need for rest may change. Listen to your body and your spirit to decipher the kind of rest you need. Make that a priority as you plan your time, knowing that time is a valuable commodity not just to the world, but to you as well.

TO ALL THE PEOPLE YOU CAN

As you finish this stage of your life, the relationships you've made have added to the memories you take with you. Friends have entered your life, shared meaningful events, and left you a more vibrant person. Teachers and coaches have given you life lessons you'll share with others. Parents, family members, and family friends have nurtured and cared for you in good times and bad. We couldn't do this thing called life without other people!

Now's a good time to reflect on the people who have had a positive impact on you. You may take some time to let them know your feelings in a phone call or text. They may not even realize they've impacted you! Now is also a good time to think about those who've had a negative impact. What have you learned from those relationships? Are you able to put any hurt behind you, or do you need more time to work on those issues? Now is a good time for that too, as we all have boundaries that need to be set for healthy relationships.

During the next stages in your life, you will meet a lot of new people. You will have chances to make new relationships, learn new things, and grow. Take the lessons you've learned from past relationships along with you, both good and bad. Your job is to seek out the relationships that nurture your soul, that feed your curiosity, that allow you to be the best possible version of you. Understand that setting boundaries with people in your life is necessary to create the space you need for yourself.

Writer and activist Adrienne Maree Brown, author of *Emergent Strategy*, has a lot to say about relationships and the power of good in the world. One of the lessons of *Emergent Strategy* states, "There is a conversation that only the people in this room right now can have. Find it." What a powerful, yet intimidating statement! Imagine the possibilities if you could have a deep conversation with each of the people with whom you come in contact—so

much good would come of that! If you were able to match skills, to debate intellectually, to cook up new and interesting projects with everyone in your path, the possibilities for good in the world would be endless.

GOOD ACTIONS
GIVE STRENGTH
TO OURSELVES AND
INSPIRE GOOD ACTIONS
IN OTHERS.

—PLATO

To move into a space that allows for these vital and complex conversations, you must be willing to overcome your own fears and insecurities to connect with those who may be different from you. How do you conquer the stereotypes you have for others? How do you allow yourself to be vulnerable enough to recognize your own bias and prejudice? This is a lot of work to tackle, but acknowledging and undertaking your own flawed thinking gives you entree to new relationships. And the sooner you start this difficult work, the better.

Many years ago, a group of college students were camping in South Dakota. They didn't realize that the week they'd chosen to camp was also the week of the world's largest motorcycle rally. The wilderness was gorgeous, the skies were expansive, and the engines were loud! They found themselves surrounded by people with whom they didn't feel they had anything in common. The students were in sandals, the bikers were in sturdy black boots. The students were strumming acoustic guitars, the bikers were revving engines.

One day, a student was washing clothes in the campground laundry room. Looking out the window as he folded clothes, he saw a biker in his biker leathers and dark glasses coming toward the building. It was an intimidating sight for the student. As the biker approached, the student saw him bend down to pick something up. As he resumed walking, he looked really angry.

Finding himself unsure of how to react, the student looked for alternate exits from the laundry room. As the biker came into the building, he grabbed the lid of the recycling container that sat right in front of the door. He tossed in the item he'd stopped to retrieve: a discarded soda can. "I hate it when people don't recycle when the recycle can is right there!" he explained when he saw the student's wide eyes.

The stereotype burst. Instead of a gruff, aggressive guy, the student discovered that his camping neighbor was a committed recycler, something they had in common. This small encounter allowed the student to see the people around him with different eyes. Maybe his preconceived notions of others were wrong. Maybe he should step outside his comfort zone and get to know people on a deeper level. This has served him well over the years and remains a work in progress. There is always inner work for us to do to embrace those around us more fully and authentically. Putting effort into this is good work at its utmost.

Once you are confident in engaging with those around you, you're able to have those unique conversations that Brown is talking about. You can have that exceptional connection to someone new, which can lead to the extraordinary. Who is life putting in front of you? Could it be a roommate or friend, a teacher or instructor? Life can be surprising, so watch for the good that comes out of unexpected relationships.

Stephen Hawking was known for being a world-class theoretical physicist and mathematician, second only to Einstein. Although he died in 2018 from complications of amyotrophic lateral sclerosis (ALS), also known as Lou Gehrig's disease, his discoveries and insight are still driving scientific research today. Looking at Hawking's life, there are two big lessons to be learned in terms of doing good "to all the people you can."

First, when Hawking graduated from Oxford University in England and entered graduate school at Cambridge University, there was one professor with whom he hoped to study. Hawking was a bright and promising student, and he hoped to be mentored by the biggest names at his new school. Instead, he was assigned to a different professor to oversee his graduate work.

Hawking was disappointed and complained but went ahead with his studies in cosmology. As his studies progressed, he discovered that the famous professor was rarely on campus and rarely available to his mentees. His professor, meanwhile, was there to guide and encourage Hawking as he progressed in the work on his thesis. This professor, Dr. Dennis Sciama, was pivotal to Hawking's work by providing a challenging, yet nurturing, environment for the young scientist.

Life put Dr. Sciama in front of Hawking, and it led him to immeasurable success in unlocking the secrets of our universe. Hawking thought he knew who he needed, but Dr. Sciama was there to be *the good* to his student and guided him through his graduate study. This was an unexpected relationship, but the good it led to was amazing.

> THOSE WHO ARE HAPPIEST ARE THOSE WHO DO THE MOST FOR OTHERS.
>
> —BOOKER T. WASHINGTON

While Hawking was pursuing his graduate studies, he was diagnosed with ALS and given three years to live. ALS is a progressive neuromuscular disease that affects the body, but not the mind. As his disease progressed, Hawking was confined to a wheelchair and eventually lost the ability to move and speak. Still, his mind was sharp, and he learned to do complex equations in his head. He was given technology to help him communicate and continue his research. Even though he had incredible barriers to overcome, Dr. Hawking continued to publish books and articles, engage in ground-breaking research, and address audiences around the world.

He said, "I want to show that people need not be limited by physical handicaps as long as they are not disabled in spirit." He was an inspirational figure who didn't allow even the most debilitating illness to stand in his way of doing good in the world. How can Dr. Hawking's story of perseverance inspire you to overcome barriers? What do you feel is holding you back from engaging with the people life has put in front of you and from doing good?

Doing good for others builds relationships of all kinds. Some may be transient and short, but others may impact you for many years. As we think about and practice doing good for people, we develop empathy. *Empathy* is different from *sympathy*, a word often used in sad situations. People express sympathy for someone when a loved one dies or when someone is sick. Sympathy is feeling sorrowful because of someone else's misfortune. Empathy, however, is the ability to understand

THE ONLY WAY TO SURVIVE IS BY TAKING CARE OF ONE ANOTHER.

—GRACE LEE BOGGS

someone's situation as if you were experiencing it yourself.

To put it more succinctly, empathy is active, but sympathy is passive. Empathy puts you in a position to accompany another through difficulty rather than just standing on the sidelines. Empathy is something you have to practice to be good at but allows for a deeper connection. By being with someone in their sorrow or pain, by journeying with them, you are a partner in healing rather than a fixer.

Researcher Brené Brown has done a lot of work exploring empathy. One illustration she uses to explain the difference between sympathy and empathy shows a person in a deep hole in the ground. This person has experienced something hard and is dealing with a lot of sadness. Another person comes by and realizes there is someone in the hole and that the person in the hole is sad. The person walking by calls down with best wishes and encouragement and then walks on.

Another person walks by and also notices the person in the hole. The second person climbs down into the hole and sits with the person in her sadness. The first person displays sympathy and the second person, who journeys down to be in relationship, is showing empathy. And like the ideas of charity and justice, both are necessary and good.

Empathy requires a lot of the giver but creates a relationship. Sympathy is important too and often requires less. There's even a whole section at the card store labeled "Sympathy." You can't practice empathy with just a card! But both are needed as you work to do good to people in your world.

There is a Zulu phrase that is helpful in understanding the importance of empathy to our world. The phrase uses the word *ubuntu*, which doesn't have a direct English translation. The best explanation is, "I am, because you are." Humanity is meant to be plural rather than singular. We aren't meant to walk through our lives all on our own, but to support and care for each other. That is the heart of empathy and doing good. South African Archbishop Desmond Tutu explained it well. "My humanity is bound up in yours, for we can only be human together."

You have been equipped with an education, with relationships, and with years of experience in life. As you go forward on your journey and meet new people, experience new things, and create new relationships, surprises and community await you. Life will put some interesting and perhaps unexpected people in your path. How will you greet them? What will you learn from them? Life will give you chances to dive deep with others, in joy and in sorrow. Those experiences will expand your perspective and teach you about the diversity of the world.

Each chance you have to do good will build you into the person you're meant to be. There will also be times when you allow others to do  good for you. Those are sweet and heartwarming experiences. Allow others to show you their goodness and care. As humans, we're bound together in this practice of doing good, united in our abilities to both give and receive.

AS LONG AS EVER YOU CAN

Means, ways, places, time, people … there are so many opportunities to do good in the world. And, as a recent graduate, you have a lot of years ahead of you to do it! You have dreams, big and small, to chase. Plan the steps and set your goals now, whether they are for the day or the decade, and go for it.

Have you heard the riddle, "How do you eat an elephant?" The answer is, "One bite at a time." Although we don't recommend actually eating one of these endangered animals, it's a great analogy about how we move toward making our dreams into reality. One bite at a time means planning and taking action every day. One bite at a time means perseverance and forward movement despite setbacks. In taking one bite, one action, at a time, you'll find that you make progress steadily and reliably. What may seem now like an insurmountable feat (elephants are really big!) becomes achievable in time. That will give you the confidence and encouragement to keep doing good!

There is a bridge in England that has become famous, not because of the nursery rhyme about it falling down, but because of the number of people who have attempted or completed suicide from it. The Wearmouth Bridge in Sunderland, England was built in 1796 and sits high over the Tyne River. Over time, the people in Sunderland realized that lives were being lost from the bridge. A local group posted signs on the bridge railings that read, "Talk to us, we'll listen anytime" along with a phone number.

Very quickly these signs were vandalized. Not with meaningless graffiti, but with messages of love.

Passersby added notes of encouragement and comfort. A local student, Paige Hunter, was inspired by this and added her own notes on every post of the bridge. Her notes were laminated to protect them from the weather and tied with colorful string. They say things like, "You don't want to die, you just want the pain to go away" and "You have the power to say, 'This is not how my story will end.'"

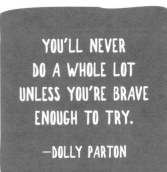

YOU'LL NEVER DO A WHOLE LOT UNLESS YOU'RE BRAVE ENOUGH TO TRY.

—DOLLY PARTON

These notes remind everyone on the bridge, whether they are just passing by or in deep pain, that they matter and someone cares. Ms. Hunter used a place as a means to do good to people through time. To date, over twenty-eight lives have been saved by this act of good in the world. That's like a whole classroom of people who have chosen life because of this simple act of love.

Doing good and reaching your goals takes a lot of heart as well as a lot of hard work. Some dreams require strong muscles, others require sharp minds, many require both! Whatever the training and education you embark upon, remember

SET YOUR
HEART JUST ON
DOING GOOD. DO GOOD
OVER AND OVER AGAIN
AND YOU WILL BE FILLED
WITH JOY.

—BUDDHA

the both/and mindset. As you embrace all the possibilities and look past the binary of this or that, you can fully actualize all that life has in store for you. Instead of seeing just binary options, you will see the full range of possibilities in front of you. Do you remember the song "Going on a Bear Hunt"? You might have learned it as a little kid or at camp. In the song, you are on a bear hunt and encounter different obstacles as you journey forth. There's a dark forest—you can't go over it, you can't go under it, you have to go through it. There's a sticky swamp—you can't go over it, you can't go under it, you have to go through it. The fun part of the song is making the sound effects for the different stages of the adventure. The fun part of this in life is expanding your perspective to take in all the options in front of you.

In adopting a larger perspective in life, you must be vulnerable and open to all life has in store for you. This allows you a bigger window in which to see where and how you can do good in the world. What does it mean to be vulnerable? The word has some negative connotations with which you may be familiar. Some meanings of the word *vulnerable* relate to being unprotected or being a sucker. But did you know that the word also means being accessible and open, being ready? Do you see similarities between the two meanings? Being vulnerable and open can be scary! It may leave you exposed to others in new and different ways, but it will also allow you to engage in doing good in new and different ways.

For many years after graduating, a social worker helped people experiencing homelessness. The organization she was employed by focused on building relationships with people on the streets and journeying with them toward housing. This required years of working through the steps of the housing process. People needed state IDs. That means they needed birth certificates. People needed income. That means they needed job training and employment opportunities. For folks without permanent addresses, getting these things was complicated. One man the social worker met became an instant friend. His name was Mark, and he was alone with a grocery cart of belongings and a dog named Bella.

Over the months they met together, they were able to get Mark the papers he needed and sign him up for subsidized housing. Eventually, Mark got a small apartment not far from where he was camping. They were both excited to move in his belongings and to know that they would still see each other frequently.

One day as the social worker was driving to work, she passed a busy corner and saw Mark with a sign that said, "Homeless, need help." She panicked and pulled into the nearest parking lot to talk to her friend. After saying hi, she asked tentatively, "What happened to your apartment?" Mark replied, "Don't worry. Everything is fine. I just like to get out and meet people."

For most, standing on a corner asking for help would be frightening and demoralizing, but it was the only way Mark knew to engage. He and his social worker collaborated on new ideas, and he decided to volunteer at a food pantry, helping people pick out the groceries they needed. For Mark, this took a lot of vulnerability, but it proved to be a way for him to find good in the world and give back to the community.

Vulnerability can mean different things for everyone. So finding these areas of growth can mean some real soul searching and honesty. That hard work will reveal more and more areas where you can do good. How do you dig deep to become more vulnerable and more able to do good in the world? Supportive and loving friends can offer a foundation of trust that allows you a safe space. Building those relationships takes time and effort, but you won't regret it. There are abundant books, films, podcasts, and articles that will challenge you on this journey. Don't shy away from those things, but allow them to uncover places you want to grow. When you find those growing edges, lean into them and give yourself the time and space to bloom there.

It's not a mistake that you are in this world, at this time, in this place. You are here to live a full life—complex and marvelous in its messiness. Your place and time and community allow you abundant ways

> THE BEST WAY TO
> NOT FEEL HOPELESS
> IS TO GET UP AND DO
> SOMETHING. DON'T WAIT
> FOR GOOD THINGS TO
> HAPPEN TO YOU. IF YOU
> GO OUT AND MAKE SOME
> GOOD THINGS HAPPEN,
> YOU WILL FILL THE
> WORLD WITH HOPE, YOU
> WILL FILL YOURSELF
> WITH HOPE.
>
> —BARACK OBAMA

and means to do good in the world.

Wesley's quote focuses on the word "do," but it also repeats the word "all" several times. Use the word *all* to approach and confront your life in ways that lead to good. That means changing the narrative at times, from negative to positive. And also remembering the both/and mindset.

When things don't go your way, it's easy to label them negatively. If you aren't selected for a job for which you applied, you may feel rejected. Instead, remind yourself that you have other opportunities to focus on. What feels like failure can become growth. What starts as disappointment can lead to new paths.

All the good in your life may not start out easily, but you can learn to see your journey in all of its intricacies as a force for good in the world. People who never stumble will never learn how strong they are. Those who haven't learned from mistakes don't become wise. Allow every experience—good, bad, or gray—to be a chance to learn and do good. Use the power of "all" for learning and growth.

You will find ways big and small to bring good into our world. Trust in the good of the world—the good you've created and will continue to create by all means, in all ways, in all places, in all times, and to all people for the rest of your life.

JOHN WESLEY

THE STORY BEHIND THE QUOTE

Born in 1703 in Lincolnshire, England, John Wesley came from a religious family, and his father was an Anglican priest. Both he and his brother Charles followed in their father Samuel's footsteps. As a student, John Wesley was intensely serious. At Oxford, he kept scrupulous diaries of his activities, meals, and prayer schedule. Wesley had a "method" for his life's daily tasks, and the movement he went on to found is called "Methodism" for a reason!

On his return trip from the rather disappointing mission to evangelize in the new colony of Georgia, the ship on which Wesley was traveling encountered a storm. While many passengers screamed in terror, a group of German Moravians sat calmly. They explained that their faith in God meant they did not fear death. Their deep faith transformed Wesley and drove him to look beyond the established church as a means of sharing the Gospel. He preached where he found people, in pastures and outside factories, empowering those who were being marginalized in industrial England. He built chapels that housed clinics and schools as well as Bible studies. Other causes John Wesley championed included the abolition of slavery and allowing women to preach. His Methodist movement was influential in early American church development, where preachers did circuit rides to visit far-flung communities.

The "Do all the good you can" quote is distilled from several of John Wesley's sermons, delivered in England during his long life of itinerant preaching. His writings reflect his deep passion for the good each person contributes in the world, regardless of their time, place, or means. His words have inspired generations to both be and see the good in the world.

DO ALL THE **GOOD** YOU CAN,

      BY ALL THE **MEANS** YOU CAN,

IN ALL THE **WAYS** YOU CAN,

      IN ALL THE **PLACES** YOU CAN,

AT ALL THE **TIMES** YOU CAN,

      TO ALL THE **PEOPLE** YOU CAN,

AS **LONG** AS EVER YOU CAN.

– John Wesley

NOTES
ON DOING
GOOD

BY ALL THE MEANS YOU CAN

BY ALL THE MEANS YOU CAN

IN ALL THE WAYS YOU CAN

IN ALL THE WAYS YOU CAN

IN ALL THE PLACES YOU CAN

IN ALL
THE PLACES
YOU CAN

AT ALL THE TIMES YOU CAN

AT ALL
THE TIMES
YOU CAN

TO ALL THE PEOPLE YOU CAN

TO ALL
THE PEOPLE
YOU CAN

AS LONG
AS EVER
YOU CAN

AS LONG
AS EVER
YOU CAN

ABOUT DEXTERITY BOOKS EDITORIAL

Dexterity is an award-winning indie publisher based in Nashville, Tennessee. We describe ourselves as "Book People with Startup Hustle," and our team, including the Dexterity Collective of seventy-plus book publishing professionals, believes in the power of books to make a difference.

From editorial development to production, strategic consulting to data analytics, and from digital-only distribution to full-service sales representation, we not only publish our own titles—we make our menu of publishing services available to publishers and indie authors everywhere.